Published by Creative Education
123 South Broad Street, Mankato, Minnesota 56001
Creative Education is an imprint of The Creative Company

Designed by Stephanie Blumenthal
Production Design by Melinda Belter

Photographs by Barrett & MacKay, C. Henderson, Images International/Erwin C. Bud Nielsen,
Jay Ireland & Georgienne Bradley, Lewis Kemper, Joe McDonald, C. Allan Morgan,
Ira S. Rubin, Kevin Shafer, Tom Stack and Associates, and Doris VanBuskirk

Library of Congress Cataloging-in-Publication Data

Bach, Julie S., 1963–
Sloths / by Julie Bach
p. cm. — (Let's Investigate)
Includes glossary and index
Summary: Examines the physical appearance, habitat, and
behavior of the slow-moving sloth.
ISBN 0-88682-613-6
1. Sloths—Juvenile literature. [1. Sloths.] I. Title. II. Series.
III. Series: Let's Investigate (Mankato, Minn.)
QL737.E2B335   1999
599.3'13—dc21   98-7856

First edition

2 4 6 8 9 7 5 3 1

SLOTHS

JULIE BACH

Creative Education

SLOTH

FACT

Sloths account for 25 percent of the mammals in the Central and South American rain forests.

SLOTH

COUSINS

Sloths are distantly related to armadillos and anteaters.

Right, two-toed sloth

Can you imagine taking two minutes to walk across a room? That pace would feel just right to the strange creature called the sloth, the slowest-moving land animal on earth. To a sloth, slow is the way to go.

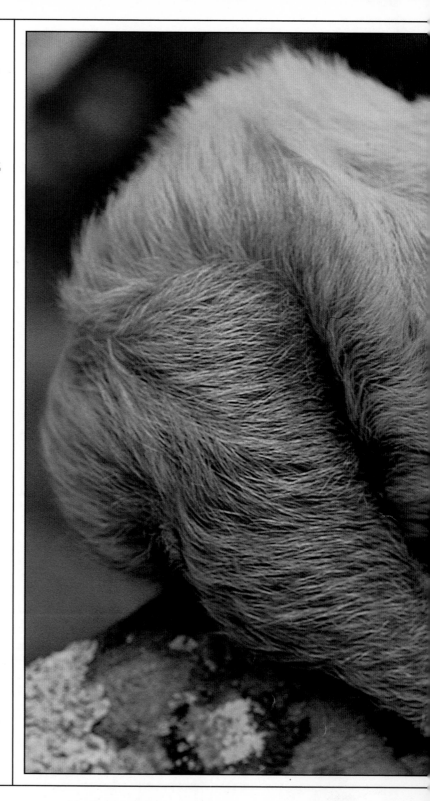

SLOTH
STRETCH

Sloths have more vertebrae in their necks than most mammals, so they can rotate their heads from side to side to see in all directions.

Above, harpy eagles prey on sloths
Right, three-toed sloth mother and young

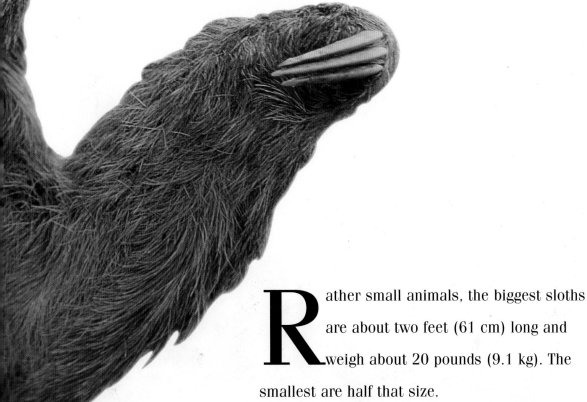

SLOTH BODIES

The name "sloth" comes from an Old English word that means "sluggish" or "lazy." But a sloth isn't lazy. Its slow movements help it to blend in with its **rain forest** surroundings and hide from other animals.

Sloths are curious-looking mammals that spend almost their whole lives in trees. This creature hangs upside down from branches with the help of curved claws that are usually three inches (7.6 cm) long. The claws are curled just right so that   the sloth can use them for climbing from branch to branch.

Rather small animals, the biggest sloths are about two feet (61 cm) long and weigh about 20 pounds (9.1 kg). The smallest are half that size.

7

Above, a ciba tree

SLOTH

FOLLY

8

S loths have small, rounded ears and blunt noses. Some species, or kinds, of sloths have a small tail; others have none. While most mammals' fur grows in a downward direction, from spine to belly, the sloth's long gray or brown fur grows from belly to spine. This allows rain to run off the sloths when they are hanging upside down.

Right, three-toed sloth

A single sloth can have 100 butterflies living in its fur, and scientists once found 978 beetles living in the fur of one sloth.

Their fur is also home to several kinds of moths, beetles, and mites. These insects lay their eggs and live in the sloth's thick fur, which is often covered with green **algae,** giving the animal a greenish-brown look. This also helps it blend in with its jungle **habitat.**

Left, brown-throated, three-toed sloth
Above, the sloth bear from India is not a sloth

SLOTH

RAINBOW

Sometimes during dry seasons, leaves in the rainforest turn yellow. The algae in sloth fur dries out and turns yellow, too, so the sloths still blend in with their background.

Above, jaguars hunt sloths for food
Right, brown-throated, three-toed sloth
Opposite, Hoffman's two-toed sloth

Sloths use their ability to **camouflage** themselves as protection against dangerous animals. A sleeping sloth looks like the stump of a branch. If walking in the jungle not knowing what to look for, a person could walk right under a sloth and never see it.

SLOTH
SIGHTINGS

Sloths are kept in many zoos in the United States, including the Hogle Zoo in Utah, the Cleveland Zoo, and the San Diego Zoo.

Above, back markings of brown-throated, three-toed sloth
Right, Southern two-toed sloth

KINDS OF SLOTHS

Scientists divide sloths into two groups. One type of sloth has three toes on its hind feet, but only two toes on its front feet. They are called **unau,** or two-toed sloths. They are about two feet (61 cm) long and are grayish brown with no markings. These sloths can be kept healthy in **captivity** because they eat a wide variety of leaves and fruit. There are two species of two-toed sloths.

13

T**he other kind of sloth has three toes on both its front and back feet. It is called **ai**, after a crying sound it sometimes makes. Ai are smaller than unau and even more sluggish. The males often have a bright yellow or orange patch on their backs.

Left, three-toed sloth

SLOTH

SNACK

Two-toed sloths kept in zoos eat mostly plants, but sometimes they will eat hard-boiled eggs.

14

Right, brown-throated, three-toed sloth

The three species of three-toed sloths feed only on the leaves and fruit of the **cecropia** tree. Because their diet is so limited, it's difficult to keep them healthy in captivity.

Sloths have some unusual **ancestors**, the ground sloths. This group of sloths lived millions of years ago, roaming from South America up into North America. Some were the size of a house cat, but the species called *Megatherium* was bigger than an elephant. This gigantic ground sloth had huge bones and a strong tail. It did not climb trees like today's sloths, but it did eat leaves, standing on its hind legs to reach them.

SLOTH
FOSSILS

Fossils reveal that, at the end of the last ice age, four species of ground sloths once lived in what is now the United States.

*Left, three-toed sloth
Above, Brazilian boy
with sloth and baby*

SLOTH
HEAT

When sloths get too hot, they stretch out on their backs and expose their bellies, which have less fur; this allows the sloth to release body heat.

*Above, three-toed sloth
Right, Monte Verde Cloud
Forest Reserve, Costa
Rica, Central America*

THE SLOTH HABITAT

Sloths live in the rain forests of Central and South America. These are the only rain forests where sloths can live. Even though there are other rain forests in various places all around the world, no sloths live there.

The **canopy**, or top portion, of the trees is home to the sloth. The trees grow close together in the rain forest, and the canopy is thick. This means that sloths can move from tree branch to tree branch without ever touching the ground.

Sometimes people in South America find sloths trying to cross roads. Many of these people kindly return the sloths to trees where they can survive.

Below, cecropia tree

SLOTH

Sloths have special networks of blood vessels called "retes" that allow them to conserve heat when the temperature drops at night.

Right, Catarata La Paz, Costa Rica
Opposite, brown-throated, tree-toed sloth with young

The rain forest is a humid, or wet, **climate.** That's one of the reasons sloths grow algae in their fur. They seldom dry out! Rain forests are also very warm. Sloths cannot survive in the cold. If the temperature drops below 80 degrees Fahrenheit (26.7° C), sloths let their limbs cool down while keeping their vital organs warm. Fortunately, the rain forest stays very warm most of the time, so the sloths are comfortable.

SLOTH
SWIMMERS

Scientists have found fossils of a marine, or water-dwelling, sloth that lived in the ocean millions of years ago.

SLOTH
CLUMSY

Sloths sometimes accidentally fall from trees. If a sloth lands in the water, it may swim a great distance before getting out and climbing another tree.

Right, three-toed sloth

SLOTH MOVEMENT

Moving through trees, sloths have been estimated to travel at six to eight feet (1.8 to 2.4 m) per minute. By comparison, the fastest humans can run a quarter of a mile in one minute.

Sloths can pick up the pace when they need to. Males that are looking for a female to mate with can travel relatively fast, and one observer saw a mother sloth cover 14 feet (4.3 m) in one minute when she was responding to cries from her offspring. That's twice as fast as the normal sloth pace.

Unlike most mammals, sloths are born with a full set of teeth and open eyes.

Sloths cannot walk or run. In the trees, they slide hand-over-hand from branch to branch, usually upside down. On the ground, two-toed sloths, just barely able to support their bodies on their four legs, move awkwardly. Three-toed sloths cannot support themselves at all. They drag themselves along the ground by their front limbs.

Surprisingly, many species of sloths are very good swimmers. Of course, they swim at a snail's pace. They lay on their backs or bellies in the water and circle their front limbs in a sort of crawl.

Left, brown-throated, three-toed sloth and young on the ground Below, spectacled caimans will eat sloths

SLOTH
FUSSY

Sloths belong to the same animal order as armadillos and anteaters, but they won't eat leaves with ants on them!

Above, anteaters climb trees too
Right, sloths use their tongues to reach for leaves to eat

SLOTH BEHAVIOR

Sloths do just about everything upside down. They eat, sleep, mate, and give birth that way (though some sloths do curl up in the fork of a branch to sleep). Sloths sleep or rest about 20 hours a day.

A sloth travels to the ground only once a week to defecate, or drop its body waste. A sloth usually leaves its droppings at the base of a tree, and it often covers them so that other animals will not know it is in the area.

Two-toed and three-toed sloths make different noises, but neither group is very vocal. Infants sometimes make a crying noise, and males make a cry or call during mating. Sloths are solitary animals; they tend to live by themselves rather than in couples or family groups.

SLOTH
NAME

In parts of South America, the sloth is called "lazy man."

Sloths climb to great heights

SLOTH
SENSES

Sloths have a keen sense of smell and touch that helps them to find food.

HOW SLOTHS EAT

Sloths feed at night, and they rarely drink water. They get moisture from the leaves they eat and from licking dew from the surface of leaves and branches. Most two-toed sloths eat any kind of leaves, twigs, and fruit that they can find. Even the three-toed sloths, which eat only from the cecropia tree, will eat other leaves and fruits when they have to.

Right, a young brown-throated, three-toed sloth eating

SLOTH
FACT

In scientific classification, sloths belong to the order Edentata *and the family* Bradypodidae, *one of the oldest animal families on earth.*

Left, three-toed sloth
Below, Southern two-toed sloth eating a hibiscus blossom

Sloths have no incisor, or cutting, teeth. They pull leaves off branches with their lips, then chew the leaves with their blunt teeth.

These calm, quiet animals have a very low rate of metabolism, which is the rate at which their bodies turn food into energy. A sloth may take up to a month to fully digest its food. Because their metabolism is so low, it isn't necessary for sloths to eat a lot.

SLOTH

THEFT

Baby sloths are sometimes stolen from their mothers and sold as pets.

Below and right, Southern two-toed sloths

BIRTH AND GROWTH

Male sloths mate with females and then leave the females on their own to raise the young. Females are pregnant for about six months. They give birth in only 15 to 30 minutes, and they do it upside down! The mother has to reach down and grab the infant before it falls to the ground.

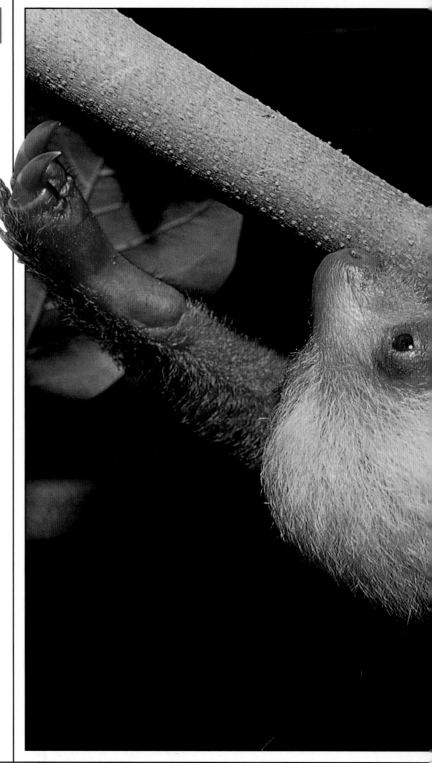

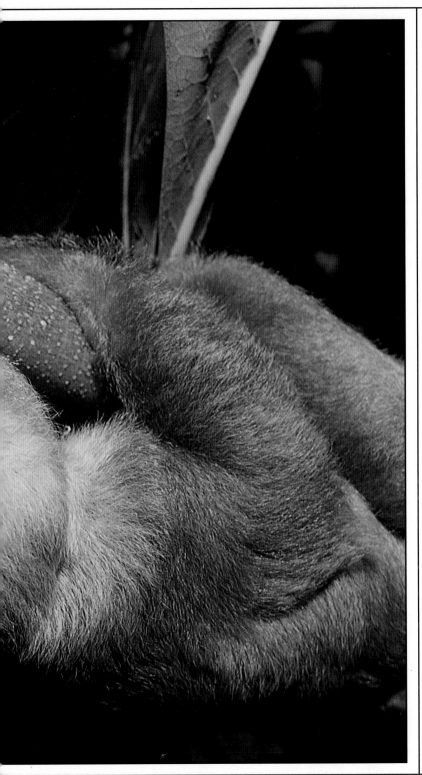

Sloths have only one offspring per year. When the baby is born, it uses its tiny claws to climb onto its mother's belly. It clings to her fur for the first month of its life. During that time, the mother protects her baby and feeds it. After nine months, it's time for the young sloth to move on. If it tries to catch a ride with its mother, she will nip it to make it travel on its own.

Sloths live for about 10 years. Their grip is so firm that they sometimes remain attached to the tree branches after death.

MYTH

Sloths must be stupid because they are so slow.

TRUTH

Research indicates that sloths are intelligent and curious.

SLOTH

28

SLOTH SURVIVAL

Sloths share the rain forest with many unusual creatures. Some of them are the sloth's natural enemies. These **predators** include large snakes, harpy eagles, jaguars, and caimans (a type of crocodile).

Right, Monte Verde Cloud Forest Reserve, Costa Rica

29

S hy creatures, sloths tend to move around only at night. Their main protection is their camouflage. They blend in with the forest so well—and they move so slowly—that predators often don't see them. They are most vulnerable when they go to the ground.

Even when they are attacked, sloths often survive. They can defend themselves with their sharp claws. Also, their heavy fur and thick skin make it difficult for other animals to injure them. Sloths also heal amazingly quickly. They can survive injuries that would kill other animals.

Left, squirrel monkeys Above, sloths have long claws for climbing

SLOTH

IMPOSTER

A large bear that lives in the jungles of India and Ceylon is called a sloth bear because it moves very slowly, but it is no relation to rain forest sloths.

SLOTH

FACT

Sloths have less muscle mass than most mammals. That's one reason their metabolism is so slow.

People who live in the rain forest do not often hunt sloths. Hunting them is usually a waste of time. Since sloths cling to high branches even after they die, hunters are not able to retrieve them.

Sloths are not considered an **endangered** animal, but their numbers are dwindling. Every year, lumber companies and farmers clear thousands of acres of rain forest with fire and bulldozers. Without the trees, sloths have no natural habitat.

Sloths may seem lazy, but these shy, gentle creatures are an important part of the rain forest **ecosystem.** Like all animals, their presence teaches us about unique and exciting areas of our world.

Glossary

Ai is the group name of three-toed sloths.

Algae are tiny, green, plantlike organisms that live in water or in wet conditions.

An **ancestor** is a relative from whom another species or person is descended.

Camouflage is a way of hiding by appearing to be part of the environment.

The **canopy** is the top portion of trees in a rain forest.

An area's **climate** is the average type of weather determined over several years.

Animals kept in **captivity** are pets or are part of zoos or parks.

A **cecropia** (si-KROW-pee-uh) is a type of fast-growing, short-lived rain forest tree that has leaves one foot (30.5 cm) across. The sap yields a latex rubber; the fruit is tube-shaped with soft, sweet flesh and many small seeds.

An **ecosystem** is a group of plants or animals living together. Ecosystems can be large, like the whole world, or very small, like a pond or forest.

Endangered animals are threatened with becoming so few in number that their kind will die out completely and disappear from the earth.

Remains of plants and animals that have turned to stone over millions of years are called **fossils.**

A **habitat** is the place where an animal or a plant naturally lives and grows.

Mammals are animals that feed their young with milk from the mother's body and whose skin is covered with hair or fur.

The chemical change that occurs when the body uses food as energy is called **metabolism.**

Predators are animals that hunt other animals for food.

A **rain forest** receives more than 100 inches of rainfall each year. It is made up of broad-leafed evergreen trees and has a warm, humid climate.

Unau (yoo-now) is the group name of two-toed sloths.

Index

blood vessels, 18
camouflage, 10, 29
ears, 8
eyes, 21
diet, 14, 22, 24
  drinking, 24
feet, 12–13
  claws, 7, 29

fur, 8–9, 10, 16, 29
  markings, 12, 13
groups
  ai, 13
  unau, 12
habitat, 7, 9, 16–18, 28, 30, 31

climate, 18
hunting, 30
life cycle, 26–27
  birth, 26
  growth, 27
  death, 27
metabolism, 25, 30
movement, 4, 7, 17,

20–21, 23, 29
head, 6
  swimming, 20, 21
noses, 8
  smell, 24
predators, 6, 10, 21, 28, 29
relatives, 4, 30

ancestors, 15, 20
sleeping, 22
teeth, 7, 21, 25
voices, 23
weight, 7